Merge with the river

Poetic Matrix Press
Madera, California

Acknowledgements

Thanks goes out to: Cynthia McFann for her friendship and dedicated computer work. Penny Otwell for her newfound friendship and her wonderful artwork. Christine Loberg for the fun photo session. Ed McCormick, Amanda Stone, Ed Whittle and Jo Maiorano for reading the manuscript and sharing their feelings. Mary Ellen Wilson for her graphic work. And family and friends for their support through the years.

copyright (c) 2004 by James Downs

ISBN: 0-9714003-2-6

All rights reserved. No part of this publication may be reproduced or transmitted in any form or by any means, electronic or mechanical, including photocopy, recording, or any information storage and retrieval system, except for personal use and in critical articles or reviews, without permission in writing from the publisher.

Requests for permission to make copies of any part of the work should be mailed to:
Poetic Matrix Press
John Peterson, Publisher
P.O. Box 1223, Madera, CA 93639
559.673.9402
e-mail: poems@poeticmatrix.com • www.poeticmatrix.com

Designed by Mary Ellen Wilson of Cavanaugh Enterprises
Printed in the United States by
The Graphic Overflow
(619) 261 6459 • (619) 231-6679
mew@emediapartners.com • mew540@sbcglobal.net
www.emediapartners.com/portfolio

Dedication

*To my friend and compatriot
in poetry, John Peterson*

*On our way, we meet people
who confirm our path
or move us along it. John
is one such person.
Over long discussions about
this life, we have found
similar beliefs of what it is
and where it should be going.
It is an affirmation that is
full and hopeful and wild.
And that we are all in
this thing together. I am
indebted for the part John
has played in moving me along
my journey. Following
are poems for you, the reader,
intended to resonate along
your path.*

*The world is girded under by the wild. The wild is in everything.
The wild is not inherently good or bad; it just is. If we each tap
into this wild, we can be part of something so big as to not
be able to see the horizon. And that is good!*

*James downs
Yosemite, california
2004*

Table of contents

I. "Do you wonder..."

I've been	3
Rhythm	4
Short sweet walk	5
Impression	6
Drawing on	6
This side of green spring road	7
"Driven deep..."	8
"Steep in..."	8
Green	9
Substance	11
This	12
Bounce	13
Wide bench	13
Someone's burning	14
Waiting for the light to change	15
Source	17
Releasing	18
An old silence	19
Peaceable kingdom	20
Smoke signals	21
Become	22
Submerged	23

II. "You got to be..."

Moon over tuolumne river	27
Next to me	28
Observing the continuum on the river's shore	29
Essential	29
At rest an hour before sunset	30
Hawk temple aerie	31
Guerilla poetry	32
Backyard boogie now mountain riverbank	33
Without falling	35
"Those who do not learn from mistakes of the past ..."	37

Table of contents

Evolve 38
Regret 40
In a contest 40
Waiting 41
A making 42
Slick 43
"Water drops..." 45
"Leaf floats..." 45
Weather 46
Frequency: to bashō 47

III. "Take heed..."

Curl 51
Bubbling under 52
Theodore roethke 53
Nighthawk's cry 54
Bait 55
Mecca 57
Grace 57
Too many choices 58
Poetry 59
Something tells me i should go 60
Bless the source 62
Sorry 62
Plunge 63
The golden mean 64
Thoughts on a real magic kingdom 65
"Thousand leaves..." 67
"I enter naked..." 67
Rain on cameron lake 68
"Arm sweeps..." 69
"Sandals in sunset..." 69
Make it last 70

Table of contents

IV. "Those were the days..."

The days 73

V. "To which god..."

The dancer 83
Lighter than 84
Parchment 85
Thanksgiving 86
Ticket to ride 87
Breathless 89
Deer in the distance: at river's edge 90
Standing watch 90
I splash my feet in 91
Geese river 92
In real time 93
In this world: a reverie 94
It's live 96
Rain 98
Possible 98
Sprout 99
Soil 100
Pacific ocean 101
Quietude a melding 101
String 102
Bio 104
Front cover artwork 104
Back cover photo 104

Merge with the river

poems by
James downs

I

"Do you wonder
why the reeds are here
at the water's edge?
They are waiting for
the wind to touch them.
They are full of
passion. Listen to
the breeze shake them
and you can hear it."

— from the movie *"Red Corner"*

I've been

On a clear   thick blue
morning in the mountains
weaving
between slick new trees   trying
to soak in
        existential
philosophies among the branches
sun rises
every day
and casts rays
'cross cliffs so one can see
stop
        realize
                yeah
in these mountains i've known
the truth
all along the way   woven between

Rhythm

Rhythm thm rhythm thm
rhythm drum drum rum da dum
hear it   hear it:

in wind   in bird's repeated
scolds   in cold stream
rushings   there
in sun's risings   settings
in breeze   a breeze brushing
inside you   you know it
FEEL it on your
skin   rhythm thm   bears it
into your eye   drum drum rum da dum
it's always
                      there   standing by
when you hear   listen here

and everywhere   rhythm thm
rhythm thm drum drum
                      rum da dum

Short sweet walk

Walk and at the end of
such a short sweet walk
find the wild as

it hovers at edges
        peripheral-vision-wiggling
a joyous raucous chaos
        wells from within
each of us on this walk
        attaches to the wild
at the point where we can
        ride it forward   where it rides us
forward   wild goes out there and
        back on trail we're
on   in us on trail we're
        on   we are   on and on
running with deer   galloping
        with bear   soaring
with eagle   growing
        with tree   slowly
slowing   slowly   slow slowing
        back out again

peripheral-vision-wiggling
a short sweet walk
out of breath now
        but won't let go

Impression

Across the long bone
of mountain   two wing

span shadows circle   slowly
twice around   soon follow

the bone   spine of mountain
until they disappear   imprint

still on my skin

Drawing on

            — to bobbi

Woman drawing
naked   in tune with
the earth   drawing

the earth to her
canvas   sweet
strokes on paper

This side of green spring road

Uphill into the mountains
i climb
passing through rolled
foothills
covered over with tall
yellow   sharp
grasses close by
grounded
green rounded trees
artistically
arranging themselves around the
hillocks
journeying on uphill
i climb
still higher to the
mountains
                into the dark shine
                of quarter
moon

Driven deep smell of
        new spring rain like: animal –
danger – wild – forest

Steep in gully-down
        down spring mountain's waking side
side of snow sleeps steep

Green

Water's edge opens door   driven ducks pile in
flaps down   waving wings madly
they settle in   brown mottled mallard stands

on water   flaps wings   like
a banner waving proudly   her
mate's head   silent smooth guarding sheen of

blue-green   they chatter importantly
yellow or brown bills   dipping water   like
experienced well-dippers in the country

his plumage proud   her tail coyly wagging
and they drew from the green of the water

orange feet tread along water's edge
wider river spot for them to paddle
around   if the water's edge closes

a door   decisive ducks pile out a window
and they drew from the green of the water

a man and a woman drop part way
up the bank   to lay out and sun
they listen to wind in trees and

water ripples on   she stretches
her arms contentedly to sky   like
a kite ready to fly   into

green-blue   they chatter importantly
she in brown-billed cap and naked to the waist
he whispers in her ear   he's plumed with

green-blue garb proudly   her tail coyly wagging at him
and they drew from the green of the water

bare brown feet pick over rock to water's edge
and dip their toes in   like newly experienced waders
they go in and out doors and

windows continually   a limb brushes limb
and they drew from the green of the water

and they drew from the green of the water

Substance

    — at the airport bookstore

      I found you
sitting on the floor   books
      scattered 'round   your legs
folded 'neath you   poet neruda
      centered
your focus   your goal
      searching
for his poem about the lobster
      that certain   substance
one of the essential
      food groups   may i
get down on the floor with you?

This

This flying bug lands on
the middle line of the last stanza of
"workshop" the poem i'm reading out of
selected and new poems by billy collins   this tiny bug
lands there just to investigate the black ink
on the stark white paper   or is he trying
to share this poem with me   work it out

with two-brained
teamwork   anyway
i'm pretty certain he doesn't know doom
is waiting at stanza end   for   soon
i plan to close the book

since i know this little future
i will gingerly pop the poem page and send him
up and read again   as this

poetry in motion   flies

Bounce

Father skipping
      with young daughter
hopping to sounds in their minds
      they bounce into the building
as he holds her little hand

Wide bench

Mother walks her child
along a bench   he giggles
whole way as she swings him

bench-end to bench-end
she ends it with a big
hug   their river is wide

Someone's burning

Sit at round blank small table
on second floor heaven
poetry room of city lights books

look out the window at pigeons and
someone's laundry   hung out
to dry   nervous eyes   the pigeons

look about and rise to the bleating
of fire sirens   someone's burning
house   it's a ritual thing

pigeons   don't see me   their backs to
building   blazed by sun   but i
snuck our books of poetry

onto the shelves   among so many
other magicians   alchemy spins
something's gone to gold   and fire

Waiting for the light to change
— a fantasy

Above the world   one can
see forests for trees
bunched in   tightly held clumps they

venture off down valley   marching
as if to sea   to see the world
isn't that what posters used to say?

through tree-eyes the world
would look a different place   especially
from those so newly uprooted and suddenly

mobile   some would stop in san francisco
in awe   all the buildings taller than they
and such a bustling around their dirt-freed

roots   one could stand on market street
talking with a stately 50 foot pine   waiting
for the light to change   exactly how

does a tree negotiate power lines?   must be
some sort of dipping dance   with leaves
a-rustling   what a dance to see   but

you'd probably also notice a yearning
rising in the sap   an indecision   a longing
to be in the mountains   on our journey

to the sea

Source

Words are in the river
floating up from the bottom
last attached to substantial
rocks   the words bob between
waves   we see glimpses
of sentences in our mind's eye
but we don't own the words
the river only gives them up
on loan   if we cup our hands
just right and dip in just
so   and catch them as they float
on past   in this interim we are
allowed to jumble the words
scramble the words and delight at
sentences through sight that comes upon us
in the long run   words
sink back into the river   until
someone else cups their hands just so
for a gifted loan   the words are in
the river   the river is keeper
of words   and takes them
all the way back to the open sea

Releasing

Blackbird   splashbath in
standing water   snowmelt

robin brownchest   soft shoe 'cross
snow patches   on the way to

exposed meadow   receding winter   all

pecking on the underneath
insect seeds   nourished streaks

of of of   life life life

An old silence

An old silence
waits on an
old old shelf
each day goes by
we surround
ourselves with
sound   we keep
a racket going
we're afraid to
pull that silence
down   we don't
want to listen or
we'd soon be
trapped into
sounds
of the ages:
the old silences
on old old
shelves

Peaceable kingdom

Today i came upon a red-tailed hawk
he stone sits on stone   and
steel-eyes mice a mile away
you'll get no tone from this beast's mouth
a silent searcher of his mountain home
so as he lifts off south and flies far away
it is i who sits and cries and moans and gawks

Smoke signals

Somewhere a reed vibrates
somewhere in a muggy soft night
a saxophone blows
pushing out all
the air and soul it's got   only
to suck all essentials
back in again
oh yeah that man has something to say!
truth is   he has to say it   just like
breathing or lighting a cigarette
just like quenching thirst   now
somewhere in the same quiet darkness
someone else is listening and if she drinks
it in   she'll say "that man must
know my soul"   and if she's smart
she'll put out her cigarette   put on a coat
go out into that muggy night
               and follow that music down

Become

I seem to be one
small part   yet a whole
unto self   sitting on a seat
in a corner   with a vast
unable to comprehend
size universe
i get up and open a door and
it of course opens
on another and yet another
opens out to the full
blue universe   becoming
i am always becoming
within the act
of becoming
either seated on that chair
in the corner   or standing
by that door   turning
the shiny knob

Submerged

At the mouth of a crying creek
as it empties into thick river   a double

knobbed log submerged   green flutes
of river weeds wave   in the waves

two sets of weeping pines curve
over the mouth   like a bower   or

an entrance/exit sign   beckoning you
to stay

water rolls on deep

II

"You got to be
a spirit. You can't
be no ghost."

-from the movie *"Bulworth"*

Moon over tuolumne river

The sky is still blue
the river   blue
the moon remains blue

mountains have skin of alpenglow
grown over them   this glow
goes to the river and reflects in purple rows

places like these   the wild
nears the surface   roiling up
like fine fish through tender ice

the wild runs under
the world   it suffices
in those deeper places

the sky settles into a paler sky
the river reflects a new setting sun
the moon is still blue

Next to me

Million mosquito racers   slate
back and forth
on the river   above   squadrons

of blue dragonfly   dive   bomb
skittering surface insects   under
water   seven three-inch trout

in current scooping oncoming blue
algae   closer still   inch-long
trout   no longer than the end

digit of your finger (hence fingerlings)
so young   you can see   through
to their insides   nibble food

near my toes   this
continues   all this
next to me

Observing the continuum on the river's shore

> — experimental poem

Deer	lying in sun	naked
as me	out in our wild	attentive
big	ears flicking	looking
around	observing continuum	sun
beats	on their shoulders	as mine

Essential

> — a refrigerator magnet poem

But would some
shadow play
                for
love whisper
moist fast   chant
it cool   will
part friends

At rest an hour before sunset

Amid summer wave of
heat   six umbered eared grebes
under sky blue splashes

in clumps of beach-pebble browned
grass   revealed by
      fast receding river's edge

so recently an underwater
ledge   and with dark-palmed
heads under wing

amid pulsing heat   they wait to sing
sand praises of the world
again   tomorrow   once

one will chew his back
to smooth the cypressed feathers
dry

yawning river ripples
        heat dissipates
                exhausted grebes sleep
            in groups for safety
                    black burnished heads under
                  sky splashed wings
each one sleeping out his own dry loam dream

Hawk temple aerie

      Hawktempleaerie
nested bits   twigs of lore
      journeys of just moments jammed together
more bare bones scattered as leftovers
      yin/yang/yin/yang
            bird shadow flips by
    overhead ceiling folds over
the buddha kneeling is silent about all this
     racing the moon   inveterate
flap flapping like prayers in wind
    upraised to insistent open
        babies' mouths   needs

Guerilla poetry

Gets the juices flowing
back into the streets
leaves book on park bench and
then someone picks it up   and
holds it   clutches it to
his chest   just to keep his heart
warm

Backyard boogie   now mountain river bank

It feels like my backyard   only
bigger   my long-haired mutt poodle   jacques and i

scooted through the grass like we were stalking
distant deer   yet here is where they
grazed all along   we'd huddle   blackdog and i

against a wood rail fence   so cats crawling
atop couldn't see us   until we jumped up and

scared their world   here i come
upon a treeline fence   but can't see
what might jump out to scare me   with the

perspective karma gives   i'd hug that dog under blue
skies or scold him just as i'd been treated that day   now i

sit in a vast wild blue waiting for a larger
hug or scold from father time   that's so mine
like my backyard with the statue of my mother prowing

through a waterfall   or where through anger we
buried my mother's cigarettes and lighter by her pool   as

cancer took her away   today i sit and look upon
a body of water journeying down
stream   i sift my hands through sand

and what other psychological jolts might be
buried there   i walk in the river   up

stream causing my own wake   a prow of
myself   it feels like my backyard   only

much much   bigger

Without falling

Upper vistas
granitic rock outcropping
sit and let my mind

soar   it flies along
as the river winds
as the river winds around

i can see below
the waters flow
alpine willow branches bend

down to the edges on
the horizon   crags
and sky touch   i can

sail   silently
let my mind be
part of it all   from

this high up i float
with the sense it all
fits together   a perfect puzzle

it turns
this way then
that   bending through

a sun coming up
we all want to fly
in this life without falling

> "Those who do not learn from mistakes of the past
> are doomed to repeat them"

Santayana in his classroom
    yale kids in philosophical rows
and he happens to turn and he
    happens to look
        out the window
(he knows)　all he says is "what
    a beautiful day　beautiful
day"　so he walks out the door
    and he never comes back
and that's the way it is about that
    he knows　as he goes　he knows

Evolve

The river makes a curve
if you got in a woven basket
and let the hot air take you
aloft   it would be like
a horse's neck trembling

down this low   blunt sounds of current
jut out like adolescent elbows
or old folk's bony knees

the higher you go
the curve becomes feminine
like your lover's soft skin
above her uncovered shoulders

from high above
the river curve dots into
a language mark
a question answered by
all that surrounds it

and highest yet it
is a singing road
calling out possibility
on the land

but this is just the poet's
mind   the curve is majestic
through no cause of its own   other than
tiny adjustments washing away amid
grand geological shifting   on earth
the river settles on a course   and curves

Regret

— reminiscence for connie

"I caught a salmon once (she lives in
a bay area) but i had to let him
go 'cause i caught him with a barbed
hook it was right under a golden
gate" and a tear rolled down her cheek
as she envisioned a steak of him sizzling
in her skillet

In a contest

In a contest to see who
was farthest
strongest
highest
the little boy with his dad
chunk stones
into the
river
as if they were trying to give
the entire earth back to
the open
sea
one rock at a time and
as fast as
they
could

Waiting

"I'm waiting   on the beach
for someone to come   oh

i don't know   anyone" and
with a questioning quizzical
puzzled frown upon

his face   he jumped
into his future   and came down

empty   no one knows
what   will   happen
only what has and what

is   do we want
to be islands   or

continents of
people   pushing   prodding
milling   trying

to come home   emptying
only lets the now rush in

that much faster

A making

Smooth over rub down
rough edges
television beams-in
patterns of dots   not life
once   pride and hope
fulfilling

while on the outside
animals live on that fine
edge   either ledges
or chasms   to choose
scrapes and scraps
make them   there's no hedging
there is a texture to
what they are   each day
they dance on the
razor's edge

Slick

He raises
his great gray
feathered head
as if out of
a hundred year's
sleep
rip van winkle of
the forest   and
yawns   a sigh
down through
the trees and through
his body
he had dreamed of
small gray mice
and   other   scurrying
things   running
frightened by the
wild flap of his
inevitable
wings
his   liquid black
eyes see
little things
in the distance
he takes his
time   all the
time in the world
yet   in a corner

of one unblinking eye
a gleam
as if the moon
shines
a beam between
intertwined branches
upon him
a glimmer that
he too
this great gray
feathered thing would
one day
swoop down
into the dust of
the earth

Water drops stairstep
        rocks powerfully forever
polishes them smooth

Leaf floats down cool
        still river water   i drink
from small fruit juice jar

Weather

                In the world there is a wind
                in the wind there is a world

it must be sent into the midst
of bells clanging out
the heart of the people   it takes only

one to start   that is enough
for one plus one plus   becomes

a gale that blows across
the earth   it clears
cobwebs   so

                in the wind there is a world
                in the world there is a wind

let 'er ring!

Frequency: to bashō

This slow monk   with his
stick and his bag and dirty sandals

goes on   ever on down the roads
he goes   and becomes

through his shuffling movements
in the noonday sun   he pulls

one moment of life from the fabric
for each step he takes   and his

slow methodical steps are
in rhythm of his heart   and his heart

is tuned to the world   i often wish
i could be that way   only i'm selfish

and wouldn't want to stop to take
pen in hand and write it down again

no   i'd rather that my striding gait
roll out my inner poetry   automatically

III

"Take heed: worthless
shards of pottery. He
adds one small piece
and another   and another
and another.   Is he
still not here   labor upon
labor   beauty upon beauty?"

— from television show *"Kung Fu"*

Curl

Deep smell of rain   you feel down to
bottom level   fills your lungs
tender shoots sprout from new leaf

points   they shoot from your hands   pointed to
primeval lands   smoke   curls above chimneys
manned to keep people warm   clouds

mist-over   valley in worn gray
river sands roll   taking in
scentedraindeepsmellyoufeeldownto

Bubbling under

What i can't talk of
is there   bubbling under
a waterlife right at your

fingertips   to dive below
swim below   to the bottom
is another kingdom
there washes clean
the wide mother-under   tide
softly beats our skin
washes clean and clearly sees
lifetimes within instants
what i can't talk about
is there   in that
wide deep blue bubbling-under

Theodore roethke

Roethke rooted in his green
house   finding FATHER and other
big things   he must have run the aisles

a million times after workers gathered
tools   and trudged out to put them
in their place   he must have shaped

dust into mounds   miniature king-
of-the-hill   come-and-get-mes   until he
heard his FATHER'S footsteps   roethke

rooted in a green
house   finding FATHER and other
big big things

Nighthawk's cry

        — a sonnet

Nighthawk's cry
moves outward into the world
it would be outside   for
nighthawk crawls across world's sky
making circles surrounding you   and i
moved this way from the first   circular
for all is of the same   and each
is of the all   in the frame that is
the world   though predator eyes it   the world
just is   nighthawk keeps circles
surrounding you   something outside moves
inside   yet moves me outward into the world
      and there   light reaches my eye
      despite the booming nighthawk's cry

Bait

Two fishermen flipping lines
out over water   over
and over again   making that

filament sing   making fake
fisherflies   alight
and jerk them back again

alight and jerk   alight and jerk
lightly flitting surfaces
with tempting allures

and the fish see them   it must be
dinnertime and their sure
shimmering bellies are empty   and

along come fisherfellows with
talk of food   "oh
don't go for them" i say

"it's only these fakes
these cons   these flibbetegibbets"
but who am i to speak

how many times have i looked
up at radiant surfaces
seen something with such allure   when

i was hungry or just plain bored
and bitten down   hard   taking
the bait   hook line and sinker

Mecca

Light is thinning
as i lay in the sand
each hand swerves
out perfect angelwings
the sun is thinning
out its light as it sings
lower on its horizon
the earth is turning
east   always

Grace

Tiny white flowers stretch
singular thick pinetree roots extend
cutback into waterfills
past surface
into depth's pace all its own
a kind of grace
drunk full riverhome

Too many choices

If i wasn't sitting here

i'd be sitting someplace else

having a conversation

with someone i would

not have met if i was

here instead   but i

would not have seen

a trio of iridescent

blue-green ducks fly

in formation to land

in unison   living sea-planes

causing new wakes upon

the water   if i was there

deep in conversation

Poetry

Once the experience   is

(presents itself)   ART

is change: it changes
you   you change

IT (and i don't
know what i'll:

be NOW)

Something tells me i should go

They are working so hard   struggling
rubbed raw (blocks of life within)   on
jagged stone   something told them

to leave their rich pacific foods
and come back here   old home
week   instinctual memories

too strong to resist   new life
waits   they must not be
late   the waters worn thin

in spots   they whip their tails and arch
their glittering backs and fling themselves
against the gates   let them pass   let them

pass to exactly this right place
address book correct   so
here is where they mate

and die   they lived a deep
pacific ocean life   so they've
come home

to float upside down   white gulls
stand on dead salmon   like floating
logs   and pick at rich and juicy

morsels of these scattered lives
their bones stand at beach edge
like trees   and gulls call

each other
"let's fly   free"
revived by these being's self-
sacrifice   and under rocks

tiny vibrating eggs wait

Bless the source

Water drops down
this mountain   less and less
at the source   a drying
is taking place   expressed thus:
when there is no more water
there is just no more glistening
from the mountain's face

Sorry

I scared up a duck
who slept in the reeds
she flew away and i'm
left to say
              "sorry"

Plunge

First my ten fingers   then
two flat palms   then wrist
isthmuses   then thick
forearms   and finally the abrupt
turn of elbows   this way
i plunge my arms
bit by bit through the filament
of this river surface   into

a world   where taking chances
dances in the deep   a world
where dream blossoms from
a kind of water sleep   in this
world   it clears when naked
beings appear   a world opened
as the deep wild kiss
sails   a world where
buoyancy and thickness of oil
prevails

i pull my hand   slowly
reluctantly   back
through the filament

The golden mean

Too far   across
spring   the soaring duck

sighs   duck days go
by so quickly

flying across horizons
the sun-glistening duck
could be the golden mean
for ducks before

or after   any other
time is just a shadow

of the duck soaring   too
far across spring

Thoughts on a real magic kingdom

Imprint   of deep deer tracks   in wet
sand   pair of ducks   redheaded diver
dives   and black-and-white patient floater

follows   paddling near land   trickle sound
a creek makes when it touches   rock-under-water
i search again   there they are!   eight deer on far

bank   seen through two trees   range along
ahead for food   three choose to see what
this side brings   long brown legs picking   'cross creek
one animal   at a time   passes
in a line (i am silent stock still) by me within
arms length   they see   and their big ears turning

search for real enemies   they know that i
am not one   then they graze   nipping
new green grass bundles   one gazes

his big black eyes search   always reach out
the reaching never ends   with green shoots
sticking out his mouth   the three move on

aways   i take this opportunity to step to
the creek   and spy the other five
lying in a tall grass rest   up bank from

water's edge   i sit and write all this
on a rotting log   that makes everything
wet   and i remember also the snowy white

ballet of an egret   as it too settles
within tall grasses   long neck aloft
needle-like tail feathers   flaring back

like fir-ends   and of a sudden all is aloft piercing
forward   like white flint arrowhead   on a long
search   always reaching   the reaching never ends

Thousand leaves in breeze
    buddhist bells ringing   silence
that follows   deafens

I enter naked
    midnight moon   noonday sun   and
sense always   deep light

Rain on cameron lake

Rain on cameron lake
    with rocks not quite
opaque   beneath surface

where leaves have fallen on it
    drops make interlocked
circles with the water

fog floats above these   waters
    coming by rock colored trees
upside down like a mirror

angles different here
    we must touch smooth surfaces
of rocks   peer more   back up where

water is for earth's sake
    water circles
disappear into water

Arm sweeps in under
    water   hand cupped   bubbles burst
from my fingertips

Sandals in sunset
    sand   throw shadow 'cross to
farside river shore

Make it last

I told them to go on without
me   i was drawn to this one
filament of tricklet spring

rubbing over five green
stalks of grass   i had to stop
they kept pulling on my arm

tugging at me as if
where they were going was
so important   yet

this little scene kept me
in my shoes   i reminded them
that their journey was

important   but so
was mine   only my
journey takes place without moving

IV

"Those were the days my friend
I thought they'd never end
I thought we'd laugh
forever and a day"

— from the song *"Those Were the Days"*

The days

Clearest sharp music
as american dipper bobs
beneath cold blue water   of the river
our hands hold water for an instant
yet   wetness seems second skin
without and within   so
small gusts of wind   bring
branches together and away
again   it's as if
trees clasp hands   searching
for the water   all search
for that water
music swells again   it's a forest music
from deep within   it's a water music
that comes again and again
if lucky   forest goes right down
to the river   one sees haze off mountain
granite   down long chute of water
american dipper skips along
water's skin before she dips in
she plays to music that comes
within her breast   best music   brightest
music   sharp and
clear she chirps
waits to hear an answer   where
hands hold music for an instant

there's a road   dusty   sand-rutted
off into nowhere   curves   stand here
and look off into distances
not seeing   but match roads up to roads
i imagine   one wonders if forests
have secrets   wonders will they match our dreams?
thick underbrush plays a zigzag game
standing here we could remember a childhood
name we gave it   and only when
one puts feet in dust   and touches underbrush
one just has to go

৯৶

the river gives off a different sound
at night   there are silences
not explored   music not
played through   darkened bends
colder still at night
the river dips and wends   all living things
fold their breath within   for to breathe is
to share rhythms of others   to share
in the river currents   in dark   one sees
sometimes clearer than sunblind bright
a single piano note echoes off close banks
first a swirl   then unknown things swim

colder still at night   secrets breathe out
silence grins

॰॰

in morning   drowsed birds abrupt awake
stretch   and shake dew-slaked wings
they are birds of many species   they start
talking   chirping   whistling
greeting words for us   as well as
others   and we could say the same in
first seeing you   as you get up
move around   start your day   small streaks play
and warm   your clean hair and shoulders
so if pondering birds can talk of yesterday
all can share a sense of time   sky bound
canyons   echo   with these sounds
a different key of music
a shared kind   day starts how it may
the days are coming in

॰॰

blue cold tinkling notes of one trinklet
water stream   it has searched around in
deep forest   rolling through echoed green

it tries to find its source   a water kind
it knows   goes on and on   until it empties its sound
into that larger blue-green

৺

there's a slow   jazzy   beat   within
lush meadow   being there   sitting
there   it's corralled in
by straight   tall lodgepole pines
between two of these   a lone
sharp-eared   mule   deer
marches 'cross that bigger beat
there is rhythm   as she makes her
way   there is rhythm in making any   way
she stops to   eat   one shoot
of green

৺

sky-meadow builds by layers
geology of lives   stored
in a full forest   first-tree stands
for something   tentative
animals scramble over
sentinel trees searching   soon

thousand birds thicken the sky   land
on granite walls   down which
river water falls   play of these
tree – animal – bird – wall – water
goes on   and oh a symphony swells
to   hold the water in the hand
an instant   one senses
the days are coming in

ঞ

watching sun set by the river
river thinks back to source
source thinks to beyond
beyond the swash
       of tide and pull
beyond the sky
       from longer ago
each successive tide
       sprays from folk tunes
the sun knows
       where it has to go
sun finally sets by the river
as the days come in
       as the days come in
cold   clear   blue

❧

lone american dipper chortles tunes
in bristling cold wind   brusque
pinned to clouds of gray space and moons
dipper falls silent   leaving wind to sing
we sing what we can sing
dipper dips again in sound   as wind fades
she says   hey   i'm here   here
i'm still here

❧

many streams converge in our minds' dream   we've tucked
water   in many places   impossible to remember
where it all   is
birdsong   keeps us   lifted
to higher   branches   we can see miles
away there   a bass chord of remembrances
all streams of past have their place where
we only need catalog them   to see
on banks of these separate dreams   is bitterroot
bittersweet   a chord that stretches out
of sight   remember   birdsong keeps us lifted   so we
tie this chord in tops of green trees   winch it up
there   and as many streams converge   water pools

as a body of remembrance   we see
a dipper fly through each passing thought

ঌø

there is old growth to deep forest
many hymns made to it   as
there are many hymns coming from forest leaves
old growth still here   in cold and clear
on the river   on the river
water seeks good water as the days
come in

V

"To which god shall I pray today? I'll pray to a god who whispers 'Listen to the rain hitting the sidewalk. Listen to the whistling teapot and the barking dog. Listen to everyone breathing the same air together. Sit down. Listen.'"

—Sy Syfransky,
editor of the *Sun*

The dancer

I

Coyote trots around
spins   does what pleases
him   he'll fade to shadow
as need be   but for now
does a little jig   that's big
left foot right foot left
all the way 'round the park

II

i had danced no dance until
i saw coyote choreographing
between the trees

Lighter than

Breathing oxygen takes
concerted effort   gulping in

air   lighter than
itself   standing under wet fir

branches   breathing   watching
sleek gray squirrels scampering

watching squealing raccoons
waddling   breathing-in

the world that moves
through sweet lighter-than air

Parchment

Chinese poem placed
on bamboo cart   smoothed there

to read again
and again   i come back

to it whenever i can   paper cracks
so i will just look at it

leave things to be—
come what they will

black stroke marks on parchment
and i reach a thousand times

and i'm still reaching   chinese poem
on a bamboo cart   and i kneel

on a rolled-out mat nearby

Thanksgiving

Brooks bubble-up in streams
warm sounds bank off walls   teams
of duck with iridescent blue and green wings   fly

in formation   designed to reach a southern goal
let out calls to show where they've been   why
on shoals of airstreams are all the places

we've been   fruit falls not too far
from the tree might be a sadness   but there can be
planted future-bearing seeds from what

we mean   meadow grasses sigh
unseen are the days that reach
for the all within each one

warm sands bank back and forth the walls
we give thanks for what we've seen

Ticket to ride

> "She's got a ticket to ride...
> but she don't care"
> —The Beatles

Haven't caught that
last boat yet
haven't seen it chugging nearer

from its distant dark horizon   oh
i've seen it take others
away across the sea: mother

father cousin aunt uncle
grandparents and still others i
did not know or even meet

and yes a couple of tiny
bittersweet times i thought
the boat with its slick dark sides

was here to present me
with my ticket but it
was false alarms   medical ships

come to sew me up and
send me out again   sometimes
i stand on this shore and gaze

way out to sea wondering when
will i see that dark thick smoke?
but just now i much prefer

to turn and walk away
back into these wild and bright and
exciting lands

Breathless

I became the toad
by the road only to jump

into a butterfly and sail
past the ear of a coyote

so i trotted along into
him down the trail where he

stopped to toy with a field mouse
and i dove down the tunnel into

him and lay there breathless
only to later come out and sit

by the side of the road
right next to a toad drying in the sun

Deer in the distance: at river's edge

Deer in the distance   browsing
choice tidbits   to nibble and
nourish   a part of the painting
moving the painting

now called "deer in the distance"
and the leaves above her
move as if from within

Standing watch

Fawn flicks her tail
mom stands watch   while
chewing leaves

everyone watches   and
everyone leaves

I splash my feet in

I splash my feet in
cold cold river   it continuously
pushes this way   that
feet naked to the
pulses   pushes   the waves
move past me   past me
past me somehow   i nearly
go with it   but i will
stay here and watch now
for i know the tides   the tides
the tides come   forward
and back   swept up
on our inner shores   more
to it   centered river vibrates
like a tuning fork   touched
to earth's core   i splash
my feet   in river cold beats
and earth vibrates
waters once more

Geese river

I look up   surprised
to see three geese   bountiful
black long curving necks   ending in

white bonnets and black beaks   rocking
back and forth as they mutely
swim up river

they turn and stop at a bank
to turn up bugs   this trio
of hungry angels

one on the bank lifts
her neck on high
looking   white-bottomed birds of grace:

the irony of it you want to see
geese in flight   but then they would be
gone   swimming one at a time in a line

wings folded back along sleek and sassy bodies
you sense they know of things
you will never see in your time   but

oh to witness world-curving necks!   they fly
in a ballet of white and black
and call out to each other "geese river"

In real time

There was a splash back on
the river and i didn't

see it   my head deeply
buried in a book of

poems by wislawa szymborska
flowing on her own river of words

with szymborska circling
in my head   especially

the one about the end
and the beginning   i look up

only to see the circles on the
water where the splash

had taken place

In this world: a reverie

I know:
we will make everyone be poets   they will have
to find notebooks and pencils and pens and places
to sit   and they will spend their time writing poems
working on poems   making poems   and the bombs
will stay in racks and the planes will stay in hangers
and all the people of the world won't automatically
know what poetry is   so they will have to ask each
other   so there will end up lunches where they break
bread only not heads   and they will end up sharing
their ideas and their knowledge and their food   and
they'll give treatises on poetry to each other and
histories of poetry and of themselves   and each and
every person of the world will get an idea   something
they can write about   something they can know or
imagine   and the people will get excited   and those
who can write will take down the words shared by
those who can't or can't see the page   and the people
will discuss "oh   did you think about this?"
or "how about that?"   and the time spent editing
these new friends will take each other to
their favorite places to sit and work on the poems
and make the poems better   and in this time
the soldiers would stay in their barracks editing too
and they might share a poem with their sergeants
and sergeants might open up and share with them too
and everyone in the world would work hard really hard

on poems   and those without places to sit and write
would go to places of those they met
and at a far side of a time all these people would be
gathered into huge spacious gathering places
moscow square   the vatican   tuolumne meadows
times square   tianamen square   and each
and every person now a poet would read their poem
or speak their poem   and we'd hear all the wonderful
voices   and in such a grand sharing we'd know:
it is all the same voice

and the planes and bombs and barracks would be
pressed into clean sheets of paper upon which to write
each   new   poem

It's live

To the dance
to the dance
to the dance   dance   dance

some say it is a dance
of death   and we salute
and march off in rhythm
that speaks of bullets and mad pursuit

some say it is a dance
of self   and we twirl
in a circle round and round
ourselves   getting dizzy in the head

some say it is that wild
dance   wild   and all nature's young float 'cross
the floor   hop   skip   and jumping

more will whisper that it is a dance
of love   and we will stop   the only beat
left is of our two hearts conjoining

i say it is another dance:
deathselfwildlove   rolled
into a mambo   of life   and so

i say to life:
to the dance   dance
dance   LIFE   dance

may i have this dance?

Rain

Rain filters down through
    tall dark trees
large drops part leaves
    on their way down   down
to me   here on this ground   but i
    was looking up

Possible

Burdened tree releases its snow
it had no place to go   but down
around my feet   dreams stop
coming if you think too much
about them   determined tree shifts it's
snowy weight
                      and lets fly

Sprout

On a road through wild
forest doings   movings   rootings   a cheerful
blueful   bluegray rah rah day bursts

up through pavement we are hurrying
across   hungering across   as if
blue flowers sprout from behind our wheels

as we take off and fly   our
automotive steel dives between
one lake wave and the other   sub-mariners

to the source   basic things bubbling
up out of the ground   sounding like
popcorn   percolators   underpinnings

we keep going on   at that place where
doors open   windows fly up
and if we're smart   we stop   get off

that road and let a poem sprout
wild   like ground-cover-evolving-lodgepole-
pine-fire

Soil

It gets down to   topsoil
plants growing   food
and whether we will share

it with each other   in these
cold winds   whipped by some
huge brushing back and forth

we forget   sometimes   harsh winds
and times   but a loaf of bread
is still a loaf of bread   and arms

around us are still arms
and who will we share
them with   each other   isn't it rich

this topsoil?

Pacific ocean

Wild deep blue mother
        sweeps swath   covers my feet
draws me back within

Quietude a melding

Birds on the wing and
        astronauts sing their praises
of this whole world thing

String

I have come to this water's edge
        a pledge of sorts to
strenuous wilderness strivings
        a ritual of belief in
particles of
loam   wave   breeze   dirt

        this is my church
ever wild earth   waiting
        for strung-together
day-mysteries such as
        jay caw questions   such as
fish jump concentric circles   such as
        below   the big plates shift   such as
this whole patch of dirt
        twirls the sun   our roots
sunk as deep as they can go
        on a line from here to there and back again
on this wild ride the earth is bucking
        and we have our 8 seconds
to hang on   and when we finally
        fall off   it will be in slow
motion and we will see doors
        open wide and the mysteries
strung together like
        a fine necklace of pearls... so

i come again and again to the water's edge

Let us be like colorful fishes
in the beautiful river   glistening
in the sun   with the taste
of sweet water in our mouths

Bio

James Downs lives and works in Yosemite National Park, California. A native Texan, James moved to the golden state in 1993 and happily calls himself a 'permanent Californian'. James produces a twice yearly on stage writer's night, WORDS. James has produced a number of hand written chapbooks and has published a chapbook, *Where Manzanita*, with Poetic Matrix Press. In his spare time James reads copiously, roots for his sports teams loudly, participates in as many poetry readings as possible and hikes all over Yosemite. He also intermittently teaches a poetry class for the children of Yosemite Valley School.

Front cover artwork

Penny Otwell painted **River with Alyce,** o/c, 22" x 24" in 2003 when the Merced River was at it's peak runoff. Otwell is a 40-year resident-artist of the Yosemite area who paints in oil, watercolor and acrylic. See more of her work (and the work of others) at www.yosemiteartists.org.

Otwell says, "The Sierra Nevada is the perfect place for a landscape painter. I continue to be inspired by nature and by mountains especially. Some people respond to my work through my use of color, but I am responding to what I feel about these remarkable places found here."

Back cover photo

Christine White Loberg is an active Yosemite photographer and can be reached at yosphoto@sierratel.com.

www.ingramcontent.com/pod-product-compliance
Lightning Source LLC
Chambersburg PA
CBHW020916090426
42736CB00008B/664